Rules, Regulations, and Responsibilities

DEBATING
THE ISSUES

**Rules, Regulations,
and Responsibilities**

Alcohol

JOHANNAH
HANEY

Cavendish
Square

New York

Published in 2014 by Cavendish Square Publishing, LLC
303 Park Avenue South, Suite 1247, New York, NY 10010

Library of Congress Cataloging-in-Publication Data

Haney, Johannah.
Alcohol : rules, regulations, and responsibilities / Johannah Haney.
  pages cm. — (Debating the issues)
Includes index.
ISBN 978-1-62712-407-2 (hardcover) ISBN 978-1-62712-408-9 (paperback) ISBN 978-1-62712-409-6 (ebook)
1. Drinking of alcoholic beverages—History—Juvenile literature. 2. Alcoholism—Juvenile literature. I. Title.
HV5066.H355 2014
362.292—dc23
2013031818

Editor: Peter Mavrikis
Art Director: Anahid Hamparian
Series design by Sonia Chaghatzbanian
Production Manager: Jennifer Ryder-Talbot
Production Editor: Andrew Coddington

Photo research by Alison Morretta

The photographs in this book are used by permission and through the courtesy of:
Front cover: graficart.net/Alamy.
Alamy: Bill Bachmann, 2-3; Photos 12, 19; Martin Thomas Photography, 22; Julian Clune, 25; Chris Ballentine/Paul Thompson Images, 32; Denise Hager/Catchlight Visual Services, 36; wonderlandstock, 42; Nucleus Medical Art, Inc., 43; Jamie Grill Photography/Tetra Images, 50. **Associated Press**: David Jones/PA Wire, 10; Alden Pellett, 27; Jay LaPrete, 29; Marion R. Walding/The Tuscaloosa News, 33; Phil Coale, 34; Charles Rex Arbogast, 40; Andrei Pungovschi, 45; Larry Crowe, 47; PRNewsFoto/National Institute on Alcohol Abuse and Alcoholism, 53. **Getty Images**: William Reavell, 9; Natalie Fobes, 15; Joe Raedle, 54; Michael Siluk, 56. **Superstock**: Glasshouse Images, 1, 4-5; Don Landwehrle, 6; Image Asset Management Ltd., 13, 17.
Back cover: Gyro Photography/Amana Images/Alamy.

Printed in the United States of America

Table of Contents

"Cheers!" A groomsman raises his glass of champagne and toasts the happy couple at a wedding. A church congregation consumes consecrated wine in a sacred liturgy. Friends clink beer bottles on a dance floor for a twenty-first birthday. Business associates share a bottle of wine to seal a new partnership.

On occasions like these and others, alcohol is an important part of culture throughout the United States and the world. Its use in celebration, religion, medicine, and everyday life can be traced back to ancient civilizations. However, the abuse of alcohol can lead to grave consequences for individuals and families, and alcohol-related accidents claim many lives each year.

The consumption of alcohol is rooted in controversy. The question becomes: how can people enjoy alcohol while minimizing its potentially damaging effects? The answer is not easy; it involves regulating laws surrounding the use of alcohol. Some people believe these laws should be more strict, severely limiting alcohol use in our society.

Many celebrations are a common setting for consuming alcoholic beverages. Alcohol-related laws aim to help balance enjoying a good time while keeping people safe.

Others believe they should be more lenient, giving people the freedom to make their own decisions about alcohol use.

Before examining all of these issues, it is important to understand what alcohol is and how it affects the human body.

What Is Alcohol?

In general terms, alcohol is an organic compound with many applications. Some forms of alcohol, such as methanol, are used in industrial settings in fuels and as solvents. Other types, such as isopropyl alcohol, are used in the medical field to kill germs. You have probably encountered this kind, known commonly as rubbing alcohol, if you have ever had a shot at the doctor's.

The type of alcohol discussed in this book is **ethanol**. It is used in personal care products, medications, and alcoholic beverages. The ethanol found in beverages is created through a process called **fermentation**. During fermentation yeast changes sugars, often in grains or grapes, into alcohol while releasing carbon dioxide into the air. Have you ever baked a loaf of bread? This process is also an example of fermentation. Yeast in the dough makes the loaf rise as carbon dioxide bubbles form. Beer, wine, and liquor are all fermented beverages, but liquor has a higher alcohol content because it also goes through a **distillation** process. When the fermented liquid is heated to a certain point, the ethanol becomes a vapor, and the water left behind is discarded. Once the ethanol vapor is cooled, it condenses back into a liquid that has a higher concentration of alcohol.

The yeast in this beer brew causes fermentation. The bubbles in this photo are evidence of carbon dioxide being released as the fermentation process begins.

What Happens to Alcohol in the Body?

When a person consumes an alcoholic drink, part of the beverage is broken down by enzymes in the stomach. Some ethanol is absorbed through the stomach lining, while the majority is absorbed through the small intestine. The amount of time it takes for absorption varies. If there is food in the stomach, particularly food high in fat, the alcohol will reach the bloodstream more slowly. On the other hand, absorption is faster when the alcohol is carbonated, as it is in champagne or when it is mixed with a carbonated liquid such as a soft drink. Once the alcohol reaches the bloodstream, blood pumping through veins and arteries carries it throughout the body quickly.

Usually a woman will end up with a higher level of alcohol in her blood, or **blood alcohol content**, than a man who has consumed the same amount. Women have fewer of the stomach enzymes that

Drinking excessive amounts of alcohol can have an effect on a person's appearance, including an increase in wrinkles and redness. This photo shows a composite of how excessive alcohol might affect a woman's appearance.

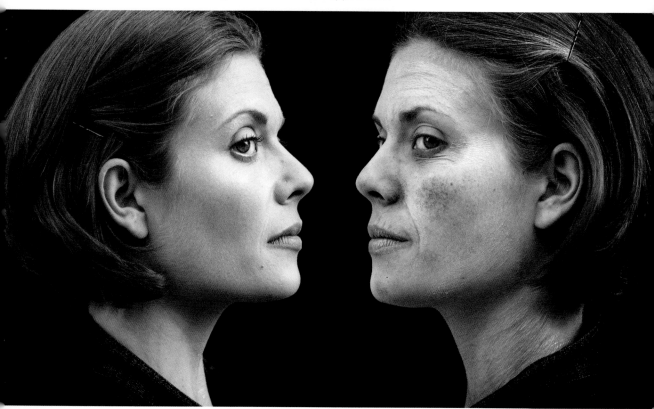

initially break down the drink, so more alcohol reaches their bloodstream. Also, the alcohol tends to travel more quickly through smaller bodies.

As the bloodstream carries alcohol to the liver, enzymes in the liver act to neutralize it. For a man of average size, the liver typically takes about one hour to process one alcoholic beverage, but each person's body is different.

How Does Alcohol Affect a Person?

Factors such as age, ethnicity, use of medications, and family history can all impact how each person reacts to alcohol. Under the influence some people will become more outgoing and social, while others will become hostile and violent.

Alcohol is a **depressant**; when it is consumed faster than the body can process it, the blood alcohol level rises and body functions slow

DID YOU KNOW?

It is just a myth that drinking coffee or taking a cold shower will make a person sober more quickly. The body will process the alcohol at the same rate regardless of the remedy—about one drink per hour.

down. Messages that usually travel quickly between the central nervous system and the brain are delayed or even stopped completely. These communications control important functions such as breathing, heart rate, and the gag reflex that prevents choking. Vision, speech, reaction times, and agility are also affected.

A small amount of alcohol will lead to a relaxed feeling as these functions slow slightly. But as the blood alcohol content goes up and the person becomes **intoxicated**, the effects on the brain and the body are greater. Dizziness and loss of balance are more likely. Expansion of blood vessels near the skin's surface leave the drinker feeling warm and looking flushed even though the body's temperature is actually decreasing. Those who drink in dangerously low temperatures, such as at an outdoor winter sports event, may think they are warm when they are actually at risk of hypothermia. An intoxicated person might experience a blackout or forget events that happened while intoxicated.

Nausea and vomiting are beginning signs of **alcohol poisoning**, which results from ingesting large amounts of alcohol in a short time period. Worsening symptoms, such as breathing trouble, unconsciousness, and seizures, can lead to a coma or even death.

Alcohol Through History

The use of alcohol can be traced to the Stone Age through artifacts; containers for beer dating back to 10,000 BCE have been found. Throughout history alcohol has been an important part of daily life. It has been used for pain relief and medicinal purposes, as a source of nutrition for lacking diets, and even as a substitute for water when there was none clean enough to drink. From offerings of alcohol to deities to the use of wine as a symbol in religious ceremonies, alcohol has also played a central part in many religions. The ancient Egyptians felt it was so important that they buried alcohol in tombs with their dead for use in the afterlife.

This ancient Egyptian statue of a brewer is evidence that alcohol has been part of human culture for thousands of years.

OIL AND ALCOHOL DO NOT MIX

In 1989 11 million gallons of crude oil damaged an entire ecosystem along the coastline of Alaska, and alcohol may have been to blame. Joseph Hazelwood, captain of the *Exxon Valdez* oil tanker, had a few evening drinks before heading out to sea. Later that night he left two crew members at the wheel and went to his cabin. They failed to steer the vessel on course and struck Bligh Reef. From the torn gash in the tanker's hull, thick sludgy oil poured into Prince William Sound and eventually spread along 1,300 miles (2,100 km) of the coast. Imagine enough oil to fill seventeen olympic-sized swimming pools washing up on shore. The result devastated wildlife in the area. Half a million sea birds, a thousand otters, and hundreds of seals and bald eagles were killed. As of 2013, almost twenty-five years later, Alaska's coast was still contaminated by thousands of gallons of oil.

While Hazelwood was found not guilty of operating a vessel under the influence, he did admit to drinking, and tests done several hours after the accident showed alcohol in his blood. The National Transportation Safety Board studied his speech in recorded radio communications for effects of alcohol, such as slurring. They determined that his speech did exhibit changes that could have come from drinking. Perhaps had Hazelwood chosen not to drink that night, one of the worst oil spill disasters in history could have been avoided.

An oil sheen surrounds the Exxon Valdez in Prince William Sound, Alaska. Scientists have learned valuable lessons about how to clean up oil spills after this environmental disaster.

For as long as people have been consuming alcohol, they have tried to control the negative effects it can have. The Code of Hammurabi, the first known set of laws, included rules for the drinking houses of Babylonia. Ancient Greek works by Plato condemned excessive drinking. Sermons given by Puritan ministers in colonial Massachusetts preached against the abuse of alcohol.

Many countries and cultures have tried prohibiting alcohol consumption entirely to avoid the societal problems it can cause, but most of these attempts have been unsuccessful. However, abstinence from alcohol is required by certain religions, including Buddhism, Islam, and some branches of Christianity, as part of their belief system.

Prohibition in the United States

In nineteenth-century America, cities were growing exponentially, the brewing industry was thriving, and saloons were popping up across the country. Many Americans were concerned about the excessive drinking, gambling, and prostitution associated with these establishments. Employers worried about the efficiency and safety of their workers if they came to work intoxicated, and rising crime rates in bustling urban areas were blamed on alcohol.

With a return to religious ideals during this time, some saw alcohol consumption as a moral problem and encouraged others to drink in moderation or even not at all. Their cause, known as the **temperance movement**, began to spread with the support of churches and other dry groups. The **Anti-Saloon League** formed in 1893 with the goal of

Bootlegged beer confiscated during the years of Prohibition was regularly disposed of, often in drain pipes.

amending the U.S. Constitution to prohibit drinking at a national level. Their effort got the momentum it needed during World War I, when a temporary wartime prohibition act required that grain be saved for food rather than used in alcohol production. In the spirit of patriotism, Americans were willing to give up their comforts to benefit the war effort.

THE GANGSTERS OF CHICAGO

The city of Chicago had a reputation for crime long before the **Volstead Act** was passed. Newspapers carried sensational stories of robbery, arson, and murder, and corruption was the norm in politics and business dealings. The ban on alcohol provided another business opportunity for the organized crime outfits in the Windy City. With the public still eager to drink, gangs took over the complete supply chain, from brewing and distillation to transportation and storage. They even ran many of the speakeasies and nightclubs where the beverages were served.

Rival gangs were in a constant battle for control of the city's bootleg industry. The Irish on the North Side clashed with the South Side Italians and their notorious leader, Al Capone. Despite the violence, the people of Chicago actually revered Capone. He connected with them, and he used his immense wealth to give back to the city, even providing food for the unemployed in his soup kitchens.

Capone made his fortune on illegal activities, and he was likely behind much of the gang-related bloodshed, including the St. Valentine's Day Massacre. But the FBI did not have the jurisdiction to pursue him; even if it had, the FBI had no evidence against him. He was convicted of failure to pay income tax, but he was never convicted of any violent offenses.

These out-of-work Chicagoans line up for a free meal at a soup kitchen sponsored by infamous mobster and bootlegger Al Capone.

The **Eighteenth Amendment** to the Constitution was ratified in January 1919, making "intoxicating liquor" prohibited. In response, the National Prohibition Act was introduced to enforce this new Amendment. This act made the production, sale, and transport of alcoholic beverages illegal. Because it was promoted by Congressman Andrew J. Volstead, the act became known as the Volstead Act. While the Eighteenth Amendment itself was quite short, the Volstead Act was more specific about the definitions and enforcement of Prohibition.

DID YOU KNOW?

The term "bootlegger" was first used in the 1880s, because such a person hid a flask of alcohol in the top of his boot before heading to trade with Native Americans. The word was revived during Prohibition and has remained in use ever since. Today anything made or sold without permission, from movies to computer software, is referred to as bootlegged.

At the start, support and enforcement of Prohibition were strong in smaller towns but weaker in big cities, where drinking was more prevalent. Despite the law, alcohol was still imported, produced, and sold illegally from coast to coast; this enterprise was called bootlegging. Prohibition spurred the growth of organized crime, which raked in huge profits from bootleg liquor. Underground clubs called speakeasies provided a place to drink in secret, and violent gang wars resulted in gunfights and murders. With continued drinking and increasing violence, support for Prohibition declined. Many also felt the law infringed on their constitutional rights.

By 1933 Prohibition had few supporters, and the **Twenty-first Amendment**, which repealed the Eighteenth Amendment, was ratified. Control over alcohol was shifted to the state level as Prohibition came to an end. Still, nearly eighty years later the debate on alcohol continues with strong arguments on all sides. How should it be handled to minimize the risks it brings without infringing on the rights of Americans?

WHAT DO YOU THINK?

Why do you think alcohol has been and continues to be such an important part of culture?

Do you think the consumption of alcohol can be dangerous? Why or why not?

Because alcohol affects each person differently, how do you think an individual should decide when he or she has had enough to drink?

Do you think a ban on alcohol could ever be successful in the United States? Explain.

Chapter 2

Because of the intoxicating effects of alcohol, state laws help regulate the purchase and sale of alcoholic beverages. Within these laws, opinions differ about how to best manage alcohol use so that people can enjoy it in a responsible way.

Drinking Age: MLDA 21

One of the most fundamental laws concerning the use of alcohol is the minimum legal drinking age (MLDA) law, which sets the age to legally purchase or possess alcohol. Because the MLDA in the United States is twenty-one years, this policy is often known as **MLDA 21**.

Before Prohibition the vast majority of states did not have a stated minimum age, but after the repeal of the Eighteenth Amendment, each state government set its own drinking age. A few chose eighteen, but most states settled on twenty-one, which was also the voting age at the time.

During the late 1960s a debate brewed about whether the voting age should be lowered to eighteen. Young men were being drafted

Establishments that sell or serve alcohol must be diligent to follow the laws relating to the sale of alcohol, or else face harsh penalties.

into the Vietnam War yet were not yet legally old enough to vote, let alone buy a beer. In July 1971, with the ratification of the Twenty-sixth Amendment, the voting age was lowered to eighteen. In response, many states also lowered the drinking age from twenty-one to eighteen, nineteen, or twenty.

Each state had the power to make its own MLDA laws until 1984, when Congress passed the **National Minimum Drinking Age Act**. Under this new law, which was part of a broader effort to reduce drinking-and-driving deaths in the United States, each state was to set the minimum age for buying or publicly possessing alcohol to age twenty-one. States that did not comply would forfeit 10 percent of their federal money for maintaining highways. Some states chose to take the penalty rather than make the change, but as of 2013 all fifty states had a minimum drinking age of twenty-one.

> # DID YOU KNOW?
> Centuries ago English common law declared that citizens could vote and be knighted at the age of twenty-one, and that age has carried through as a milestone to adulthood even today.

Drinking-Age Controversy

There are varying opinions about the drinking age in the United States. Many people are in favor of MLDA 21 and believe it is in the best interest of young people. However, there are plenty of Americans who think that the age is unnecessarily high and that the real solution lies in education.

UNIVERSITIES TAKE A SIDE

Since 2008 many university presidents across the nation have expressed their support of the Amethyst Initiative, a growing movement that says the current drinking age is actually worsening irresponsible alcohol use rather than making it better.

The administrators feel the outcome of MLDA 21 echoes Prohibition—the law has failed to stop underage college students from drinking and instead forces them to drink in private, uncontrolled situations. Drinking games and "pre-gaming"—drinking a high volume of alcohol before a sports game or other event—result in the consumption of dangerously high amounts of alcohol in a short time. And if underage drinkers find themselves in unsafe circumstances, they feel afraid to reach out for help because they could be punished for drinking illegally.

While some groups praise MLDA 21 for reducing alcohol-related deaths on the roads among teens, Amethyst supporters indicate that there are now more deaths among twenty-one- to twenty-four-year-olds from alcohol poisoning, suicide, and accidents. Fatalities are still happening, but the age group has shifted.

The Amethyst Initiative gets its name from the Greek myth about Amethyst, a girl who angered the god of wine, Dionysus, when he drank too much. The story is a fitting symbol for avoiding the negative outcomes of too much alcohol. More than 130 leaders in higher education have given their signature for the cause.

Drinking games are popular among many college students, but may encourage binge drinking.

Supporters of the current drinking age believe it is safer. They claim that more than 25,000 lives have already been saved by MLDA 21 laws and the resulting decrease in traffic accidents and suicides. Their statistics show that there was a significant increase in death rates when the drinking age was lowered in the 1970s and a 13 percent decrease in alcohol-related fatalities among eighteen- to twenty-year-old drivers once MLDA 21 went into effect.

Opponents say these numbers are misleading and cannot be linked solely to the change in the drinking age. Road deaths that are not alcohol-related have also decreased in recent decades as cars and roadways have become safer. In addition, they suggest that the death rate may have been so much higher when the drinking age was dropped because teens would drive to a bordering state with a lower drinking age to consume alcoholic beverages and then drive home, creating an obviously unsafe situation. They called these bordering states with higher accident and death rates "blood borders."

As a result, the opponents of MLDA 21 propose allowing those eighteen and up to purchase and possess alcohol once they have passed an educational course on responsible alcohol use and earn an alcohol license. Eighteen is the **age of majority**; that is, the age at which a person is legally an adult. At this milestone a person can vote, marry, enter into legal contracts, serve in the armed forces, and be held responsible as an adult in a court of law. According to the anti-MLDA 21 movement, they should also be allowed to drink legally. Present-

This car was involved in a "blood border" crash. Four teenagers crossed from Vermont into Canada, where the drinking age is eighteen, and were involved in a drinking-and-driving accident.

day eighteen-year-olds, unlike those in the past, would have the information to make responsible choices when drinking.

MLDA 21 supporters disagree, arguing that many other rights are not dictated by the age of majority, such as hunting, driving, or renting a car. A person does not gain every adult privilege and responsibility once he or she turns eighteen. They also fear that lowering the drinking age will lead to use and abuse of alcohol by younger and younger people. They claim that because the adolescent's brain is not yet fully developed,

> **DID YOU KNOW?**
>
> The National Minimum Drinking Age Act does not actually require states to outlaw drinking among people under age twenty-one. Exceptions are allowed, including drinking for "established religious purpose," as well as in the presence of a parent or guardian, in a private club, or by medical prescription. States that include these exemptions in their laws still receive all of their highway funding.

it is not equipped to handle the responsibilities and consequences of alcohol use, even with the right educational tools.

Proof of Age

Despite the debate, businesses must still be sure they sell alcohol only to customers who are of age. If they are caught selling to a minor, either accidentally or knowingly, they can face steep fines. Some will request identification from all patrons who look under a certain age significantly above twenty-one, such as thirty or forty. More cautious establishments will ask for an ID from anyone purchasing alcohol, regardless of age. Elderly customers often complain about the hassle of these policies when they are obviously old enough to buy alcohol legally.

Those who are underage might attempt to purchase alcohol using fabricated identification or someone else's ID without realizing the consequences. The penalties, which depend on the state, can include fines of hundreds or thousands of dollars, jail time, and suspension of the offender's actual driver's license.

Alcohol Sales

In the United States, each state also sets its own laws regulating the sale of alcohol in stores, for home use, as well as in bars and

In Ohio, a scanner reads driver's license information and can be used to prevent underage drinking.

restaurants, where it is consumed on the premises. One side argues that these laws help protect people from alcohol's negative effects. Others believe, however, that people have a right to buy alcohol without so many restrictions.

SERVER LAWS

Server laws address how old employees must be to mix, pour, and serve alcohol. Some states require anyone handling alcoholic drinks in a bar or restaurant setting to be at least twenty-one, but others allow

DID YOU KNOW?

It is against the law in Fairbanks, Alaska, to give an alcoholic beverage to a moose.

employees as young as eighteen to perform these tasks as long as a manager of age is present. Many states also require workers who sell alcohol in a store to be twenty-one years old and above, but some allow employees even younger than eighteen to stock shelves with sealed containers of alcohol and place these products in shopping bags.

Some believe workers handling alcohol should be of age themselves because underage employees are more likely to sell to other minors. In this case, employers would have fewer potential workers to choose from since a large portion of the applicants for these types of jobs are eighteen to twenty years old.

ABC LAWS

Alcoholic beverage control laws, or **ABC laws**, regulate how stores, restaurants, and bars sell alcoholic beverages to people. These businesses must have a liquor license for permission to sell certain types of alcohol in a particular setting. Liquor-license laws differ from state to state and sometimes even among counties or towns within a state. There are various types of liquor licenses. Some allow business owners to sell any kind of alcoholic beverage. Others allow a store to sell only wine, for example. States may also offer temporary liquor licenses for events such as festivals or fairs.

To obtain a license, a business owner must pay a fee that can range from a few thousand to hundreds of thousands of dollars, depending on the location. The process can take a long time, and some towns have only a limited number of licenses available. Even though liquor licenses help control the lawful sale of alcohol, many believe that the price and the process restrict a region's business growth.

OTHER RESTRICTIONS

Local governments also regulate alcohol promotions and availability, as well as drinking in public spaces.

While some states allow sales practices such as drink specials and happy hours with reduced drink prices, more than half prohibit these efforts to increase business. Lower prices and a limited time frame entice customers, but they also prompt people to drink more in a shorter period.

Many regions also have restrictions on when alcohol is available for sale. Bars may be required to stop serving drinks at a certain hour, often 2 a.m. Some feel the "last call" for drinks encourages drinking more heavily before the bar closes and patrons head to their cars. Additionally, stores may not be allowed to sell alcoholic beverages on Sundays, usually for religious reasons. Opponents worry that profits and taxes are lost because customers travel to other areas that do allow sales on Sundays.

Restrictions are placed not only on how and when alcohol can be sold, but also on when and where it can be consumed. Because intoxication in public spaces such as parks, beaches, and parking lots can

Drinking alcohol is prohibited in many public areas.

lead to violence, vandalism, and littering, many such places do not allow alcohol. Local or state laws or even rules set by the organization in charge of the space may prohibit consumption. Community members sometimes disagree with these limitations and feel they should be allowed to consume alcohol in public if they so desire.

The many regulations surrounding alcohol consumption are meant to protect society and individuals from alcohol's negative effects. While these measures may be controversial, it is clear that alcohol is a powerful substance that should be handled carefully.

THE BIRTH OF THE BREATHALYZER

As Prohibition neared its end and Ford made owning a car more affordable with the Model-T, drunk driving became more of a problem. Drinking and driving was not illegal, and the only way to test for alcohol use was in a lab with a blood or urine sample. It was not the most efficient method for determining the cause of an accident at the scene.

An Indiana University biochemist named Dr. Rolla N. Harger recognized the problem and set out to provide a solution. In 1938 he created the "drunkometer," an early version of today's breathalyzer, which was portable so that police officers could run the test roadside. The driver would blow into a balloon, and the officer would combine the air inside with a chemical mixture. If the solution changed color, the person had been drinking, and the darker the color, the more he or she had consumed. Dr. Harger also worked out a formula to mathematically determine the alcohol level in the driver's blood. He worked with lawmakers to ban drunk driving, and together they made his invention the official way for law enforcement to determine blood alcohol content.

Some bars provide breathalyzer machines so patrons can check their blood alcohol levels. However it is safest to abstain from drinking completely before driving.

ON THE ROAD

Imagine yourself in the front seat of a friend's car. It is late and dark, and you're not far from home. But you notice the driver fumbling with the keys, trying to find the ignition. You know he was drinking at the party, but he says he is fine. Is it safe to let him drive? Is it worth the risk?

The rules and regulations for alcohol may be hotly debated, but one thing is clear: driving after drinking is dangerous. About one-third of all car accident fatalities involve alcohol, and many times the victims are passengers in the car or pedestrians or drivers in other cars who have not been drinking.

To keep roadways safe, laws in all fifty states make it illegal to operate a vehicle with a blood alcohol concentration of 0.08 percent or higher. Also, thirty-six states prohibit carrying an open container of alcohol anywhere in the car that the driver or passengers can reach from their seats, including the glove compartment if unlocked. This restriction applies when a car is pulled over on the side of the road, but it does not include vehicles that passengers pay to ride in such as limos, taxis, and buses.

This ignition interlock device requires a driver to breathe into a breathalyzer. The ignition will not start if the user has had a drink.

The consequences for drivers who choose to break the law depend on the state in which they are driving. The driver may lose his or her driver's license temporarily or permanently. The driver may have to breathe into an ignition interlock device before the car will start to prove that he or she has not been drinking. A few states even require repeat offenders to use special license plates so that other drivers know a convicted drunk driver is on the road.

Over the years ad campaigns have helped reduce the number of alcohol-related deaths in road accidents. Public service announcements have reminded Americans that "friends don't let friends drive drunk," even if it means taking away a friend's car keys, and that the use of a designated driver—someone who has not been drinking—helps ensure a safe ride home.

Still, drunk driving remains a serious problem. Highway signs ask drivers to do their part by notifying local law enforcement when they suspect another driver is intoxicated. A simple phone call can save a life.

WHAT DO YOU THINK?

Do you believe the laws regulating alcohol should be more strict or less strict? Explain.

Do you think the minimum legal drinking age should remain at twenty-one? Why or why not?

Is it more important to control the consumption of alcohol, the sale of alcohol, or both? Explain.

If a woman still feels sober after a couple of drinks, is it all right for her to drive home? Why or why not?

Chapter 3

Alcohol can cause lifelong problems for the human body, but it may also improve health and lead to a longer lifespan. From chronic alcoholism to reduced risk of stroke, the effects are widespread and varied. The key to the healthy end of the spectrum is moderation.

Alcoholism

When the human body depends on alcohol, it suffers from a disease known as **alcoholism**. People with alcoholism, or alcoholics, are unable to control how much they drink, and they continue to do so even though it causes health, work, and relationship problems. Alcoholics may feel such a strong need to drink that they do so in secret and at unusual times, such as when they wake up in the morning. To ensure easy access to alcohol at all times, a person may hide bottles in unexpected places in the home or in the car as well as in the workplace.

Over time the drinker will develop a **tolerance**, which means the body becomes used to the effects of alcohol and needs more and

The secret, compulsive drinking of alcoholism has a profound and devastating impact on sufferers of the disease, as well as their family and friends.

more to get the same feeling. If alcoholics do not drink, they will experience **withdrawal** symptoms as the body struggles to function without alcohol. Withdrawal can cause physical symptoms such as sweating, shaking, nausea, vomiting, and increased heart rate. There are also psychological symptoms associated with withdrawal. These may include anxiety, irritability, confusion, and depression. Alcoholics may deny that they have a problem even though they exhibit the effects of the disease.

Treatment

Alcoholism is a **chronic** disease, meaning that it lasts for a lifetime. There are options for treatment, but there is not a cure.

One common treatment method is **detoxification**, which helps patients endure withdrawal while the body clears out the remaining alcohol. For those with severe withdrawal symptoms, inpatient detoxification takes place during a stay at a treatment center or hospital. Medical professionals can then monitor the patient's vital signs and provide fluids and medications directly to the bloodstream. When patients exhibit milder withdrawal symptoms, they may go through outpatient detoxification at home. Family or friends will stay with the patients during the process, and regular medical visits will help in managing the withdrawal symptoms until they are reduced.

Some medications can help recovering alcoholics stay away from alcohol when taken regularly. Disulfiram is a drug that causes physical

ALCOHOLISM VS. ALCOHOL ABUSE

Although alcoholism and alcohol abuse both relate to problems with alcohol, they are not the same. Alcoholism is an incurable disease, and alcohol abuse is a behavior that can be changed. People who abuse the substance consume too much and more often than they should. Unlike alcoholics, they may not feel the same dependence on alcohol or suffer withdrawal when they do not drink.

Still, drinking negatively affects the lives of those who abuse alcohol. They may fail to meet important obligations for family and friends, and work or school. Relationships may fall apart because of their drinking. They might choose to drink when it would be dangerous to do so, such as when driving a car or using machinery. As a result, they could injure others and face legal charges for their actions. They may suffer some of the medical problems caused by heavy drinking, and the damage could be permanent. Even though they realize drinking has caused so many negative consequences in their lives, they continue to drink too much.

While alcohol abuse is not an addiction, outside help may be needed to stop abusing. If alcohol abusers do not change their drinking patterns, they could eventually become addicted alcoholics themselves.

discomfort—headaches, nausea, and vomiting—if the patient ingests alcohol. A medication called naltrexone prevents the good feelings the drinker used to get from alcohol, and one called acamprosate reduces alcohol cravings.

Counseling and support groups, such as Alcoholics Anonymous, can help with the psychological difficulties of breaking a drinking habit. Specialists help recovering alcoholics set goals and work to change

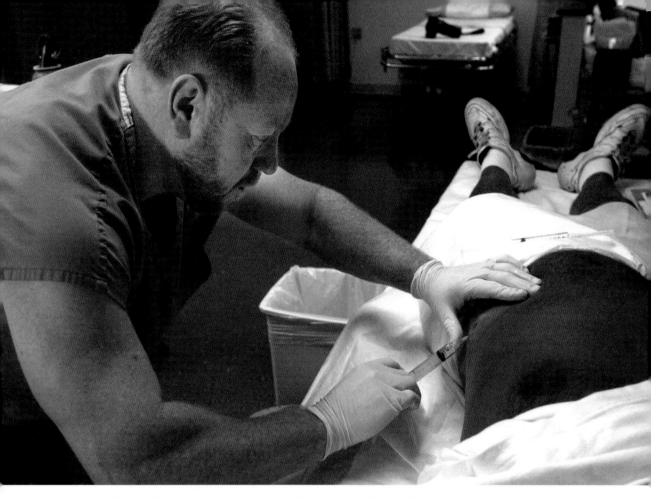

This patient is receiving a dose of naltrexone. Medication therapy is just one component of managing alcoholism.

their behaviors. Support from family members also plays a major role in the rehabilitation process.

The success of these treatment methods varies from person to person. Some will accomplish their goals and stop drinking altogether, while others will struggle between staying sober and falling back into old ways. Some will find they are unable to stay away from alcohol. The surest way for recovering alcoholics to remain sober is to avoid alcohol entirely.

Causes

The risk of developing alcoholism depends on both genetics and life-style. While research shows the disease is more common in some families than others, doctors do not yet know which genes influence alcoholism. Additionally, the presence of alcoholism in a family does not mean each family member will become an alcoholic, and some may be at risk even though there is no family history of the disease. Stress and the influence of friends could result in drinking regularly, and over time the parts of the brain that connect positive feelings with alcohol can change. The body begins to feel a strong need to drink in order to experience those same positive feelings.

DID YOU KNOW?
There have been many attempts to find a cure for alcoholism over time. In fact, Grape-Nuts cereal was originally promoted to help those who ate it to remain sober.

Health Effects of Alcohol

In addition to the risks of alcoholism, heavy drinking causes damage to the body that could be irreversible. Blood pressure may increase to unhealthy levels, possibly leading to heart failure or stroke. As scar tissue builds up in the liver, a condition called **cirrhosis**, the organ is unable to keep the blood clean of toxins. The body becomes less able to fight off infections and use the nutrients it takes in. Large amounts of alcohol can also increase the risk of developing certain types of cancer, including mouth, throat, liver, breast, and colon cancer.

RESOURCES

Alcoholics and their families do not have to deal with the disease alone. There are many resources available for information and help, including the following organizations, which have chapters in local communities.

Alcoholics Anonymous (www.aa.org): Alcoholics Anonymous (AA) is a free organization for men and women of all ages who want to stop drinking and live a sober life. Members offer support to one another through local meetings as they work through a twelve-step program to recovery.

Al-Anon (www.al-anon.org): Al-Anon offers support for families and friends of alcoholics through group meetings and individual sponsors. By sharing experiences and stories, members begin to see they are not alone in dealing with someone else's alcoholism. Al-Anon is based on the same twelve principles as AA.

Alateen (www.al-anon.alateen.org): Alateen is a division of Al-Anon specifically for teenagers. In groups led by Al-Anon members, teens discuss troubles they face in dealing with a loved one's alcoholism and offer encouragement to one another.

Adult Children of Alcoholics (www.adultchildren.org): Adult Children of Alcoholics is a group for adults who grew up in dysfunctional homes affected by alcoholism. It also uses support meetings and a twelve-step system similar to that of AA.

Alcoholics Anonymous has helped countless people on the road to recovery from alcoholism. Its method is written in the Alcoholics Anonymous *book, which is commonly known as "The Big Book." It has sold tens of millions of copies.*

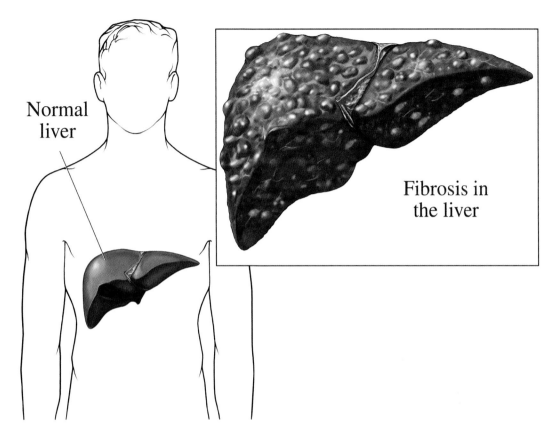

Normal liver

Fibrosis in the liver

A normal liver has a smooth surface. Excessive alcohol consumption can lead to fibrosis in the liver, which means collagen fiber deposits appear. Advanced fibrosis ends in cirrhosis.

The resulting health issues are not limited to physical ailments. Psychiatric problems such as anxiety, depression, and even suicide are possible effects of substance abuse.

Fetal Alcohol Syndrome

When a pregnant woman drinks alcohol, the fetus cannot break down toxins the same way the woman can. The amount of alcohol in the fetal bloodstream stays high for a longer period of time, and only limited nutrients and reduced amounts of oxygen are carried through. Some cells develop abnormally or even die off, resulting in a disorder known as **fetal alcohol syndrome** (FAS). FAS can cause problems throughout the body, including heart and lung defects, brain damage, and physical deformities. While there is no cure for fetal alcohol syndrome, avoiding alcohol while pregnant will prevent it completely. Drinking while pregnant also increases the risk of miscarriage, stillbirth, and sudden infant death syndrome.

Alcohol-Related Accidents

Because alcohol affects a person's coordination, concentration, and ability to react quickly, many different types of accidents can be caused by people under the influence of alcohol. Drinking-and-driving accidents are among the most common alcohol-related accidents. When a person drives after consuming alcohol, his or her ability to drive safely is compromised. It becomes difficult for him or her to concentrate on all the different elements of driving, such as steering, maintaining the right speed, watching for traffic—including bicycles and pedestrians—signaling, and managing distractions in the car like music, cell phones, and passengers. When a driver must react to something on the road, his or her reaction time is likely to be slower than if he or she were sober. Once he or she reacts, his or her coordination might not be as precise as usual. Alcohol also affects a person's judgment. It can be more difficult to determine, for example, if there is time to make a turn on a yellow light. All of these effects make driving under the influence of alcohol extremely dangerous. In fact, about one-third of all traffic-related deaths in the United States involve driving under the influence of alcohol.

Accidents involving alcohol are not limited to drunk-driving crashes. Drinking plays a role in many other injuries and deaths that could be avoided, as well. Because alcohol weakens thinking and coordination, people under the influence may make poor choices or not react quickly enough to prevent an accident from happening. Too much alcohol can

These police officers in Seattle patrol the harbor to ensure that boaters are not operating their crafts under the influence of alcohol.

also cause unsteadiness or drowsiness; a person in such a state might stumble into or sleep through a dangerous situation. In some alcohol-related tragedies, what could have been a minor incident becomes fatal. Think about how quickly you react when touching a hot burner on the stove. How much worse would the burn be if you did not pull away as soon as you felt the pain?

Alcohol is often a factor in fires and drownings, as well as in accidents involving firearms and machinery. Intoxicated fire victims may not be able to mentally process the situation fast enough to get out, and lack of muscle control may prevent a person from moving quickly to safety. Similarly, in a drowning accident a victim may slip out of a boat or fall asleep in a bathtub and be unable to keep his or her head above water to breathe or call for help. Carelessness can lead to ignorance of important safety precautions and warnings for guns and mechanical equipment. Many times the people injured in alcohol-related accidents are innocent bystanders, not the people who have had too much to drink.

Benefits of Moderation

Negative health and safety outcomes are much less likely when alcohol is consumed in moderation. But how much is moderate? The Dietary Guidelines for Americans issued by the U.S. Department of Agriculture define the appropriate amount as no more than one drink per day for women or two drinks per day for men. The number of drinks should be counted daily, not averaged over several days, and the size of one drink

All food products in the United States are required to be labeled with nutritional information. Some have proposed that alcohol be labeled with information about nutrition as well as alcohol content.

varies depending upon the type of alcohol. Twelve ounces of beer, five ounces of wine, and one and a half ounces of liquor are each considered one drink.

Research has shown that regularly drinking in moderation can have health benefits, particularly for the heart. By increasing good cholesterol and decreasing bad cholesterol it reduces the risk of heart disease, the leading cause of death in the United States. Other positives for heart health include lower blood pressure and less clotting; so the blood can flow more easily. As a result, blockages that could lead to a heart attack or stroke are less likely.

Studies also show that moderate consumption may cause other benefits, including a decreased risk of diabetes and Alzheimer's, two diseases that usually cannot be cured. When compared with nondrinkers and heavy drinkers, those who drink moderate amounts often have better mental and physical health and tend to take fewer days off work.

> **DID YOU KNOW?**
> Drinking alcohol dehydrates the body; so it is important to drink plenty of water when consuming alcoholic beverages.

They do not face as many long illnesses and consequently spend less time in the hospital. Mentally they experience less stress and depression. Some researchers claim that moderate drinkers tend to live longer.

Other doctors assert that people who do not already drink should not start consuming alcohol for the health benefits. They argue that diet and exercise can result in the same health improvements without the risks. While drinking alcohol can lead to both positive and negative effects on the body, making smart decisions about how much to consume can make all the difference.

WHAT DO YOU THINK?

Does alcoholism run in your family? What steps will you take to protect yourself from the disease?

Do you think it is wrong for a pregnant woman to consume a small amount of alcohol? Explain.

Do you think the potential health benefits of drinking alcohol are worth the risks? Why or why not?

Chapter 4

Ignoring for a moment the legal consequences and health effects, teens are still faced with tough choices when it comes to drinking. It is important to consider all the facts in order to make well-informed decisions.

Alcohol affects adolescents and adults differently, and research has shown that drinking early can lead to alcoholism. Yet some cultures that allow younger people to drink actually have lower rates of the disease. These conflicting facts coupled with peer pressure from friends can make deciding even more difficult.

Alcohol and Teen Health

As mentioned earlier, the brain continues developing into a person's twenties, and alcohol can have a lasting effect on brain functions during this period of growth. A recent study of adolescents compared brain scans of heavy drinkers with those of nondrinkers. The images showed nerve damage in the drinkers' brain tissue that could limit focus in males and visual data processing in females. Further research

At some point most teens are faced with the decision of whether to drink with friends. Weighing the pros and cons in advance can help teens stick to a personal decision.

has found that alcohol can cause the brain itself to become smaller, negatively impacting higher-level learning. Psychologists observed that teenagers who regularly drank did not do well on tests assessing their memory and attention span or while performing basic skills, such as reading a map.

Underage drinkers also are more likely to be sexually active than their peers who choose not to drink. And because alcohol consumption affects their decision-making process, teens under the influence are more likely to find themselves in risky situations, such as having sex without protection or with a partner they do not know. Clouded judgment results in higher rates of sexually transmitted disease, unplanned pregnancy, and rape among teenage drinkers.

The younger the alcohol user, the higher the risk of developing alcoholism later in life. Statistics show that 47 percent of adolescents who start drinking before age fourteen will eventually become dependent. Of those who wait until the minimum legal drinking age of twenty-one to drink, only 9 percent will suffer from alcoholism.

Cultural Differences

While numerous studies show that there are negative consequences for heavy drinking in youth, most European countries allow teens to drink. So why does it seem that they have fewer alcohol-related problems than the United States, where the drinking age is the highest in the world? This generalization is a common misconception, but it does

Alcohol and College Students— A Dangerous Mix

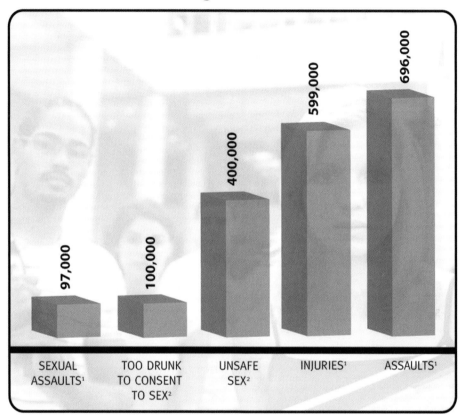

Excessive use of alcohol can result in unsafe sex practices as well as injuries and assaults.

hold some truth. Some European countries do have lower rates of alcoholism, but the reason seems to lie in the attitude toward alcohol rather than the drinking age.

In cultures where alcohol is simply accepted, rather than seen as either a toxic substance or the key to a good time, alcohol abuse is less

A HIGH-ENERGY DEBATE

The combination of alcohol and caffeine is nothing new. Bartenders have been mixing liquors with coffee, soda, and energy drinks for years. But in 2010 a sudden rise in alcohol poisoning cases and alcohol-related deaths among students in several college towns made doctors wonder. They discovered that one common factor in many of these cases was canned drinks containing both alcohol and caffeine.

As a result, the Food and Drug Administration conducted a study of these types of beverages, including a drink called Four Loko. They found that one can was the equivalent of three to four beers and multiple cups of coffee and cost only $2.50.

These beverages, dubbed "blackout in a can," enticed inexperienced drinkers because they were cheap, strong, and tasted more like fruit flavoring than alcohol. But consumers often did not realize how much alcohol they were taking in because of the stimulating effects of the caffeine. The FDA determined that these drinks did not meet their safety rules and required the companies to remove the caffeine from their products.

The beverage companies changed their ingredients to comply with the new rules, but they disagreed with the FDA's decision. They claimed overconsumption results from all alcoholic beverages, not just theirs.

Alcoholic caffeine drinks originally came under fire in part because they were thought to be marketed to a young audience.

common. Drunkenness is not the goal of drinking, and it is not socially acceptable. Because of this, people learn to consume alcohol either in moderation or not at all. For example, consider the cultural differences between France and Italy. In both countries alcohol consumption is high, but the rates of alcoholism are very different. In France, parents communicate strong opinions for or against alcohol to their children, and the society as a whole is more tolerant of intoxication. Problems

DID YOU KNOW?

A person with an exaggerated fear of alcohol is said to have a medical condition called methyphobia.

with alcohol abuse are more prevalent there than in Italy, where parents express more neutral feelings about drinking and drunkenness is frowned upon.

Stand Your Ground

Even after examining all sides of an issue, standing by personal choices can be hard if your peers disagree. Teens feel peer pressure on many controversial topics, but thinking through the many arguments and figuring out how you feel before being placed in the situation can help you stick to your own opinions. If you find you disagree with any of the current rules and regulations, make your opinions known. There are countless ways to get involved in change. Join an organization that shares your belief. Write a letter to your local government. Lead by example; make smart choices to keep yourself and those around you safe.

DID YOU SEE THAT?

You have probably seen the ads—attractive partygoers, cold beverages, and a catchy punchline. But did you know that ad agencies keep you in mind when making these commercials? Alcohol companies have chosen to follow a set of codes regarding what is in their ads and where they appear so that they target legal drinkers instead of minors.

The Federal Trade Commission provides oversight, checking that the ads are not aimed at viewers under twenty-one and that no more than 30 percent of the audience is underage. Some state and local governments also place their own restrictions on alcohol advertising, such as banning billboards near schools.

Some worry that alcohol ads make drinking seem glamorous to teens and they will be more likely to try it. Others think minors feel less curious when they see that alcohol is just another product, like shampoo or batteries.

Several studies have concluded that alcohol advertising does not increase overall alcohol sales but instead convinces consumers to choose a particular brand when they do buy. In fact, television audiences are often exposed to more alcohol onscreen during their favorite shows than during the commercial breaks. Regulations do not apply to TV plot lines now, but perhaps the issue will be debated in the future.

Billboards for alcohol such as this one must adhere to specific guidelines to ensure that they do not target people who are not old enough to purchase alcohol.

WHAT DO YOU THINK?

Should companies be allowed to sell alcoholic drinks with added caffeine, or was the FDA right to restrict them? Why?

Do you think alcohol advertising encourages teenagers to drink before they reach the legal drinking age? Explain.

If you feel pressured into drinking by your peers, how will you respond?

Glossary

ABC laws—Short for alcoholic beverage control laws. Laws that regulate how stores, restaurants, and bars sell alcoholic beverages.

age of majority—The age at which a person is legally an adult.

alcohol poisoning—A condition resulting from ingesting large amounts of alcohol in a short period of time that can ultimately lead to death.

alcoholism—A disease that keeps a person from controlling how much he or she drinks.

Anti-Saloon League—A group founded in 1893 that worked toward amending the U.S. Constitution to prohibit drinking at a national level.

blood alcohol content—The amount of alcohol found in the bloodstream.

chronic—Relating to a medical condition that is continuous or recurrent.

cirrhosis—A condition caused by scar tissue buildup that keeps the liver from functioning properly.

depressant—A substance that causes functions of the body to slow down.

detoxification—A treatment for alcoholism that helps patients endure withdrawal symptoms while the body clears out the remaining alcohol.

distillation—A heating and cooling process that results in concentrated alcohol.

Eighteenth Amendment—The 1919 constitutional amendment that began Prohibition.

ethanol—The type of alcohol found in alcoholic beverages.

fermentation—A process by which a yeast turns sugar into alcohol.

fetal alcohol syndrome—In a newborn, a group of symptoms, including cell die-off and abnormal development, related to a woman's consumption of alcohol during pregnancy.

intoxicated—A state in which a person's blood alcohol content is high enough to affect brain and body functions.

MLDA 21—Short for minimum legal drinking age 21. A policy that set the age to legally purchase or possess alcohol at twenty-one.

National Minimum Drinking Age Act—The 1984 act that required states to set the minimum age for purchase and possession of alcohol to twenty-one or lose a portion of their highway funding.

temperance movement—A campaign encouraging others to drink in moderation or not at all.

tolerance—A condition in which the body needs more and more alcohol to achieve the same effect.

Twenty-first Amendment—The constitutional amendment that ended Prohibition in 1933.

Volstead Act—Another name for the National Prohibition Act, passed in 1919, which detailed the definitions and enforcement of Prohibition.

withdrawal—A syndrome of usually extremely uncomfortable physical effects often suffered by someone trying to break an addiction to alcohol or another substance.

Find Out More

Books

Langwith, Jacqueline. *Alcoholism*. San Diego, CA: Greenhaven, 2009.

Wallace, Stephen. *Reality Gap: Alcohol, Drugs, and Sex—What Parents Don't Know and Teens Aren't Telling*. New York: Union Square Press, 2008.

Wechsler, Henry. *Dying to Drink: Confronting Binge Drinking on College Campuses*. Emmaus, PA: Rodale Books, 2003.

Websites

The Cool Spot

www.thecoolspot.gov

Through this website, the National Institute on Alcohol Abuse and Alcoholism (NIAAA) addresses alcohol use among teens in realistic terms. The site includes interesting facts, fun games, and interactive quizzes.

Drinking Age

http://drinkingage.procon.org

As part of the ProCon.org website, this page offers an unbiased look at the drinking-age argument with pros and cons presented side by side. There is also background information, statistics, and a video gallery of related news clips.

Alcoholism

www.mayoclinic.com/health/alcoholism/DS00340

This web page, which is part of an extensive health information site run by the Mayo Clinic, provides in-depth details on the disease and useful resources for prevention and support.

Index

Page numbers in boldface are illustrations.

About the Author

Johannah Haney is an author and editor living in Boston. She has written many books for young learners, as well as magazine articles. She particularly enjoys writing about science topics.